D1455874

Poetry Parade

Wishes, Wings and Other Things

Poems for Anytime

Heinemann Library
Chicago, Illinois

© 2001 Reed Educational & Professional Publishing
Published by Heinemann Library,
an imprint of Reed Educational & Professional Publishing,
100 N. LaSalle, Suite 1010
Chicago, IL 60602
Customer Service 888-454-2279
Visit our website at www.heinemannlibrary.com

Designed by Dot Gradations
Printed in Hong Kong

05 04 03 02 01
10 9 8 7 6 5 4 3 2 1

Wishes, wings, and other things : poems for anytime.
    p. cm. – (Poetry parade)
    ISBN 1-57572-399-9 (lib. bdg.)
    1. Children's poetry, English. 2. Children's poetry, American. I. Heinemann Library (Firm) II. Series.

PR1175.3.W57 2000
821.008'09282—dc21

00-023387

Acknowledgments
Alan Marks, pp4-5; David Holmes, pp6-7; Diana Mayo, pp16-17, 28-29, 30-31; Susan Winter, pp10-11; Rhiannon Powell, pp12-13; Dom Mansell, pp14-15; Valerie McBride, p16; Tom Kenyon, p18; Allan Curless, p20; Lisa Smith, p21; Mick Reid, pp22-23, 24-25; Jocelyn Wild, pp26-27.
Green Song by Judith Nicholls. © Judith Nicholls 1988, reprinted by permission of the author; **The Baby of the Family** by Wendy Cope, from 'Casting A Spell' published by Orchard Books © Wendy Cope. Reprinted by permission of the author; **The Court Jester's Last Report to the King** by Jack Prelutsky. Copyright untraced; **Supply Teacher** by Allan Ahlberg, from 'Please Mrs Butler' by Allan Ahlberg (Kestrel 1983) (pg 16, 16 lines) Copyright © Allan Ahlberg 1983. Reprinted by permission of Penguin Books Limited; **The Cheetah, My Dearest, Is Known Not to Cheat** by George Baker, from 'Runes and Tunes and Chimes' published by Faber and Faber Limited. Reprinted by permission of the publisher; **A Cast of Hawks** from 'A Bundle of Beasts' by Patricia Hooper. Text copyright © 1987 by Patricia Hooper. Reprinted by permission of Houghton Mifflin Company. All rights reserved; **Cat** by Eleanor Farjeon, from 'Silver Sand and Snow', published by Michael Joseph. Reprinted by permission of David Higham Associates Limited; **Roger the Dog** by Ted Hughes from 'What If The Truth?' by Ted Hughes published by Faber and Faber Limited. Reprinted by permission of the publisher; **Grim and Gloomy** from 'The Complete Poems for Children' by James Reeves, published by Heinemann. Reprinted by permission of Laura Cecil Literary Agency on behalf of the James Reeves Estate.

Some words are shown in bold, **like this.**
You can find out what they mean by looking in the glossary.

Contents

Pussy Cat, Pussy Cat
a traditional rhyme

Pussy cat, pussy cat,
Where have you been?
I've been to London
To look at the Queen.
Pussy cat, pussy cat,
What did you there?
I frightened a little mouse
Under her chair.

4

How Doth
the Little Crocodile
by Lewis Carroll

How doth the little crocodile
   Improve his shining tail,
And pour the waters of the Nile
   On every golden scale!

How cheerfully he seems to grin,
   How neatly spreads his claws,
And welcomes little fishes in,
   With gently smiling jaws!

Through the Jungle

a rhyme from India

Through the jungle the elephant goes,
Swaying his trunk to and fro,
Munching, crunching, tearing trees,
Stamping seeds, eating leaves.
His eyes are small, his feet are fat,
Hey, elephant, don't behave like that.

6

The Duck
by Ogden Nash

Behold the duck.
It does not cluck.
A cluck it lacks.
It quacks.
It is specially fond
Of a puddle or pond.
When it dines or sups,
It bottoms ups.

On the Ning Nang Nong
by Spike Milligan

On the Ning Nang Nong
Where the Cows go Bong!
And the Monkeys all say Boo!
There's a Nong Nang Ning
Where the trees go Ping!
And the tea pots Jibber Jabber Joo.
On the Nong Ning Nang
All the mice go Clang!
And you just can't catch 'em when they do!
So it's Ning Nang Nong!
Cows go Bong!
Nong Nang Ning!
Trees go Ping!
Nong Ning Nang!
The mice go Clang!
What a noisy place to belong,
Is the Ning Nang Ning Nang Nong!!

9

The Flattered Flying-Fish

by E. V. Rieu

Said the Shark to the Flying-Fish over the phone:
"Will you join me to-night? I am dining alone.
Let me order a nice little dinner for two!
And come as you are, in your shimmering blue."

Said the Flying-Fish: "Fancy remembering me,
And the dress that I wore at the Porpoises' tea!"
"How could I forget?" said the Shark in his guile:
"I expect you at eight!" and rang off with a smile.

She has powdered her nose; she has put on her things;
She is off with one flap of her luminous wings.
O little one, lovely, light-hearted and vain,
The Moon will not shine on your beauty again!

Little Boy Blue

a traditional rhyme

Little Boy Blue,
Come blow your horn,
The sheep's in the meadow,
The cow's in the corn.
Where is the boy
Who looks after the sheep?
He's under a haycock
Fast asleep.
Will you wake him?
No, not I,
For if I do,
He's sure to cry.

There Was an Old Man with a Beard

by Edward Lear

There was an Old Man with a beard,
Who said, "It is just as I feared! —
   Two Owls and a Hen,
   Four Larks and a Wren,
Have all built their nests in my beard!"

Solomon Grundy

a traditional rhyme

Solomon Grundy,

Born on a Monday,

Christened on Tuesday,

Married on Wednesday,

Took ill on Thursday,

Worse on Friday,

Died on Saturday,

Buried on Sunday.

This is the end
Of Solomon Grundy.

Extract from **The Bed Book**

by Sylvia Plath

Beds come in all sizes —
Single or double,
Cot-size or cradle,
King-size or trundle.

Most Beds are Beds
For sleeping or resting,
But the *best* Beds are much
More interesting!

Not just a white little
Tucked-in-tight little
Nighty-night little
Turn-out-the-light little
Bed —

16

Instead
A Bed for Fishing,
A Bed for Cats,
A Bed for a Troupe of
Acrobats.

The *right* sort of Bed
(If you see what I mean)
Is a Bed that might
Be a Submarine

Nosing through water
Clear and green,
Silver and glittery
As a sardine

Or a Jet-Propelled Bed
For visiting Mars
With mosquito nets
For the shooting stars . . .

Countdown
by Jack Prelutsky

There are ten ghosts in the pantry,
There are nine upon the stairs,
There are eight ghosts in the attic,
There are seven on the chairs,
There are six within the kitchen,
There are five along the hall,
There are four upon the ceiling,
There are three upon the wall,
There are two ghosts on the carpet,
Doing things that ghosts will do,
There is one ghost right behind me
Who is oh so quiet . . . BOO.

18

Bedtime

by Allan Ahlberg

When I go upstairs to bed,
I usually give a loud cough.
This is to scare The Monster off.

When I come to my room,
I usually slam the door right back.
This is to squash The Man in Black
Who sometimes hides there.

Nor do I walk to the bed,
But usually run and jump instead.
This is to stop The Hand —
Which is under there all right —
From grabbing my ankles.

Hush Little Baby
an African American lullaby

Hush, little baby, don't say a word,
Papa's going to buy you a mocking bird.

    If that mocking bird won't sing,
    Papa's going to buy you a diamond ring.

If the diamond ring turns to brass,
Papa's going to buy you a looking-glass.

    If the looking-glass gets broke,
    Papa's going to buy you a billy-goat.

If that billy-goat runs away,
Papa's going to buy you another today.

21

The Horseman
by *Walter de la Mare*

I heard a horseman
　　Ride over the hill;
The moon shone clear,
The night was still;
His helm was silver,
　　And pale was he;
And the horse he rode
　　Was of ivory.

Tickling

by Theresa Heine

He giggles and squeaks,
And wriggles and cries,
And curls and rolls,
And screws up his eyes,
And squirms and squeals,
And shouts and yells,
And screeches and begs,
And bangs his legs,
Till mum puts her head
Round the door and says,
"Stop tickling your brother!"

This is the Hand
by Michael Rosen

This is the hand
that touched the frost
that froze my tongue
and made it numb

this is the hand
that cracked the nut
that went in my mouth
and never came out

this is the hand
that slid round the bath
to find the soap
that wouldn't float

24

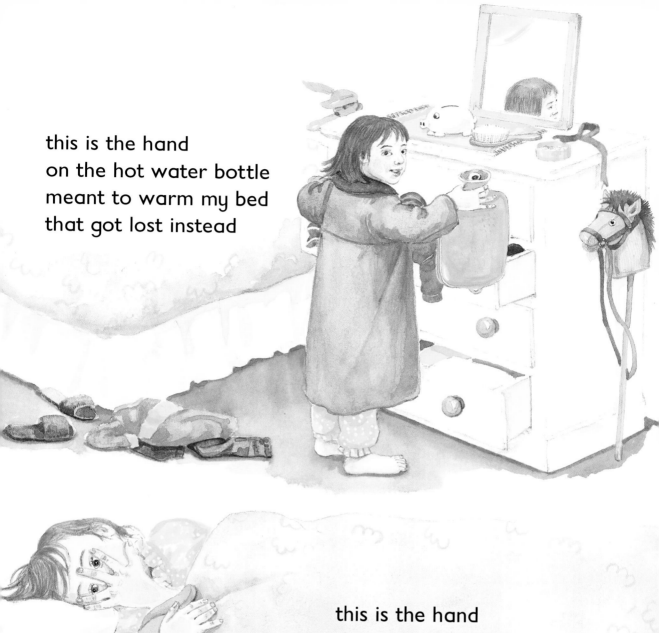

this is the hand
on the hot water bottle
meant to warm my bed
that got lost instead

this is the hand
that held the bottle
that let go of the soap
that cracked the nut
that touched the frost
this is the hand
that never gets lost.

25

New Shoes

by John Agard

Buying new shoes
takes so long.
When the colour is right
the size is wrong.

The lady asks
How does it fit?
I say to Mum
Pinches a bit.

But that's not true
It's just because
I don't want the brown
I prefer the blue.

The lady goes inside
brings another size
this time the blue.
Not too big. Not too tight.

As you guessed
Just right, just right.
Mum says, "The blue will do."
And I agree. Don't you?

Spaghetti

by Shel Silverstein

Spaghetti, spaghetti, all over the place,
Up to my elbows – up to my face,
Over the carpet and under the chairs,
Into the hammock and wound round the stairs,
Filling the bathtub and covering the desk,
Making the sofa a mad mushy mess.

The party is ruined, I'm terribly worried,
The guests have all left (unless they're all buried).
I told them, "Bring presents." I said, "Throw confetti."
I guess they heard wrong
'Cause they all threw spaghetti!

Oodles of Noodles

by Lucia and James L. Hymes, Jr.

I love noodles. Give me oodles.
Make a mound up to the sun.
Noodles are my favourite foodles.
I eat noodles by the ton.

I Had a Little Nut Tree

a traditional rhyme

I had a little nut tree,
Nothing would it bear
But a silver nutmeg
And a golden pear;
The king of Spain's daughter
Came to visit me,
And all for the sake
Of my little nut tree.
I skipped over water,
I danced over sea,
And all the birds in the air
Couldn't catch me.

If I Were King
by A. A. Milne

I often wish I were a King,
And then I could do anything.

If only I were King of Spain,
I'd take my hat off in the rain.

If only I were King of France,
I wouldn't brush my hair for aunts.

I think, if I were King of Greece,
I'd push things off the mantelpiece.

If I were King of Norroway,
I'd ask an elephant to stay.

If I were King of Babylon,
I'd leave my button gloves undone.

If I were King of Timbuctoo,
I'd think of lovely things to do.

If I were King of anything,
I'd tell the soldiers, "I'm the King!"

Index of First Lines